P9-BJQ-475

Chosen Poems
Old and New

AUDRE LORDE

W · W · Norton & Company

NEW YORK · LONDON

Copyright © 1982, 1976, 1974, 1973, 1970, 1968 by Audre Lorde. *All rights reserved.*

Some of these poems have appeared in *Heresies; The Black Scholar; The Black Collegian; The Iowa Review; Sinister Wisdom;* and *Lotus.* Others have appeared in *Black World, The Negro Digest, Seventeen Magazine, Fits, Umbra, Poetry Northeast, Parasite, Venture Magazine, Harlem Writers Quarterly, Freedomways, Massachusetts Review, Transatlantic Review, American PEN Journal, Works, Omen, Aphra, Woman: A Journal of Liberation, Amazon Quarterly, Chrysalis, MS Magazine, Painted Bride Quarterly, Squeezebox, HOODOO, Essence, Moving Out, Paunch,* and *Nimrod.*

Published simultaneously in Canada by George J. McLeod Limited, Toronto. Printed in the United States of America.

THE TEXT OF THIS BOOK is composed in the typeface Primer. Display type is Palatino. Composition and manufacturing are by the Maple-Vail Book Manufacturing Group. Book design is by Marjorie J. Flock.

Library of Congress Cataloging in Publication Data
Lorde, Audre.
    Chosen poems, old and new.
    I. Title.
PS3562.075C4   1982   811'.54   81-22484
                                      AACR2

ISBN 0-393-01576-9
ISBN 0-393-30017-X {PBK.}

W. W. Norton & Company, Inc. 500 Fifth Avenue, New York, N.Y. 10110
W. W. Norton & Company Ltd. 37 Great Russell Street, London WC1B 3NU

1 2 3 4 5 6 7 8 9 0

To FRANCES LOUISE CLAYTON

our footsteps hold this place
together
our decisions make the possible
whole.

Contents

From **Coal, First Cities,** *and* **Cables to Rage**

From **From a Land Where Other People Live**

From **New York Head Shop and Museum**

New Poems

Here are the words of some of the women I have been, am being still, will come to be. The time surrounding each poem is an unspoken image.

There are no poems included here from *The Black Unicorn* because the wholeness of that sequence/conversation cannot yet be breached.

Audre Lorde

Staten Island, New York
1981

From Coal, First Cities, *and* Cables to Rage*

---

* Some of the poems originally printed in *First Cities* (1968) and *Cables to Rage* (1970) were republished in *Coal* (1976).

Memorial I

If you come as softly
as wind within the trees
you may hear what I hear
see what sorrow sees.

If you come as lightly
as the threading dew
I shall take you gladly
nor ask more of you.

You may sit beside me
silent as a breath
and only those who stay dead
shall remember death.

If you come I will be silent
nor speak harsh words to you—
I will not ask you why, now,
nor how, nor what you knew.

But we shall sit here softly
beneath two different years
and the rich earth between us
shall drink our tears.   [1950]

Second Spring

We have no passions left to love the spring
who have suffered autumn as we did, alone
walking through dominions of a browning laughter
carrying our loneliness, our loving and our grief.

How shall we know another spring
For there will come no flower where was fruit before
Now we have little use for spring's relentless seeking
who walked the long, unquestioned path
straight into autumn's trailing arms
who saw the summer passions wither
into dry leaves to hide our naked tears.

Still Autumn teaches bearing
and new sun will warm our proud and cautious feet
but spring came once
and we have seen the road that leads through summer
beautiful and bright as clover on a hill
become a vast appalling wilderness and rain
while we stood still
racked on the autumn's weeping
binding cold love to us
with the corners of her shroud.

[1952]

Anniversary

The bitter tears are stone
but one quick breath
remembers love
and the long years you've lain
bride to the thunder
sister to fallen rain
who ate a bitter fruit
to dance with death.

We have no right to love
now you are dead
who could not hold you here.
Our tears
water an alien grass.
All has been said
and you have walked in silence
many years.

But April came today
though spring comes ever
even in the empty years
since you have slept
it was in April
that you chose to sever
young love and self
and I remembered
and I wept.

[1953]

Memorial II

Genevieve
what are you seeing
in my mirror this morning
peering out from behind my eyes
like a hungry bird
Are you seeking the shape of a girl
I have grown less and less
to resemble
or do you remember
I could not accept your face dying
And do not know you now
But surely your vision stayed
stronger than mine
Genevieve tell me
where do the dead girls wander
after their summer?

I wish I could see you again
far from me even
birdlike
flying into the sun
your eyes
are blinding me
Genevieve.   [1954]

To A Girl Who Knew What Side
Her Bread Was Buttered On

He, through the eyes of the first marauder
saw her, his catch of bright thunder, heaping
tea and bread for her guardian dead
crunching the nut-dry words they said
and, thinking the bones were sleeping,
he broke through the muffled afternoon
calling an end to their ritual's tune
with lightning-like disorder:

'Leave these bones, Love! Come away
from their summer breads with the flavour of hay—
your guards can watch the shards of our catch
warming *our* bones on some winter's day!'

Like an ocean of straws the old bones rose up
Fearing the lightning's second death;
he had little time to wonder
at the silence of bright thunder
as, with a smile of pity and stealth,
she buttered fresh scones for her guardian bones
as they trampled him into the earth.

[1955]

Oaxaca

Beneath the carving drag of wood
the land moves slowly.
But lightning comes.

Growing their secret in brown earth
spread like a woman
daring
is weary work for still-eyed men
who break the earth
nursing their seed
and a hard watch through the dry season.
Yet at the edge of bright thin day
past the split plow—they look
up the hills—to the brewing thunder
for the storm is known.

The land moves slowly.
Though the thunder's eye
can crack with a flash
the glass-brittle crust of a mountain's face
the land moves slowly.
All a man's strength in his son's arms
to carve one sleeve
into rock defiant earth
and the spread land waits.

Slow long the plowing
through dry-season brown.
and the land moves slowly.

But lightning comes.

[1955]

Gemini

Moon minded the sun goes farther from us
split into swirled days, smoked,
unhungered, and unkempt
no longer young.

All the earth falls down
like lost light frightened out between my fingers.
Here at the end of night
our love is a burnt out ocean
a dry worded, brittle bed.
Our roots, once nourished by the cool lost water
cry out—"Remind us!"—and the oyster world
cries out its pearls like tears.

was this the wild calling I heard in the long night past
wrapped in a stone closed house?
I wakened to moon and the sound breached dark
and thinking a new word spoken—
some promise made—
broke through the screaming night
seeking a gateway out

But the night was dark
and love was a burning fence about my house.   [1956]

Pirouette

I saw
your hands on my lips like blind needles
blunted
from sewing up stone
and
   where are you from
                you said
your hands reading over my lips for
some road through uncertain night
for your feet to examine home
where are you from
                you said

your hands

on my lips like thunder
promising rain
A land where all lovers are mute.
And
     why are you weeping
               you said
your hands in my doorway like rainbows
following rain
why are you weeping?

I am come home.

[1957]

The Maiden

Once I was immortal beside an ocean
having the names of night
and the first men came
with a sledge of fire
driving the sun.

I was brought forth in the moonpit of a virgin
condemned to light
to a dry world's endless mornings
sweeping the moon away
and wherever I fled
seeking a new road home
morning had fingered the harrowing rivers
to nest in the dried out bed
of my mother sea.

Time drove the moon down to crescent
and they found me
mortal
beside a moon's crater
mouthing the ocean names of night.

[1958]

Suspension

We entered silence
before the clock struck.

Red wine into crystal
is not quite

fallen
air solidifies around your mouth
once-wind has sucked the curtains in
like fright against the evening wall
prepared for storm before the room
exhales your lips
unfold.
Within their sudden opening
I hear
the clock begin
to speak again.

I remember now with the filled crystal
shattered, the wind-whipped curtains
bound and the cold storm
finally broken
how the room felt
when
your word was spoken—

Warm
as the center of your palm
and as unfree.   [1959]

Father, Son, and Holy Ghost

I have not ever seen my father's grave.

Not that his judgment eyes have been
forgotten
nor his great hands' print
on our evening doorknobs
            one half turn each night
            and he would come
            drabbled with the world's business
            massive and silent as the whole day's wish
            ready to redefine each of our shapes—
but that now the evening doorknobs wait
and do not recognize us as we pass.

Each week a different woman—
regular as his one quick glass each evening—
pulls up the grass his stillness grows

calling it weed. Each week
A different woman has my mother's face
and he, who time has,
changeless,
must be amazed
who knew and loved but one.

My father died in silence, loving creation
and well-defined response.
He lived
still judgments on familiar things
and died
knowing a January 15th that year me.

Lest I go into dust
I have not ever seen my father's grave.   [1960]

Father, The Year Has Fallen

Father the year has fallen.
Leaves bedeck my careful flesh like stone.
One shard of brilliant summer pierced me
and remains.
By this only
unregenerate bone
I am not dead, but waiting.
When the last warmth is gone
I shall bear in the snow.   [1961]

Coal

I
is the total black, being spoken
from the earth's inside.
There are many kinds of open
how a diamond comes into a knot of flame
how sound comes into a word, colored
by who pays what for speaking.

Some words are open like a diamond
on glass windows
singing out within the passing crash of sun
Then there are words like stapled wagers
in a perforated book—buy and sign and tear apart—
and come whatever wills all chances
the stub remains
and ill-pulled tooth with a ragged edge.
Some words live in my throat
breeding like adders. Others know sun
seeking like gypsies over my tongue
to explode through my lips
like young sparrows bursting from shell.
Some words
bedevil me.

Love is a word, another kind of open.
As the diamond comes into a knot of flame
I am Black because I come from the earth's inside
now take my word for jewel in the open light.   [1962]

Song

The wild trees have bought me
and will sell you a wind
in the forest of falsehoods
where your search must not end

for their roots are not wise.
Strip our loving of dream
pay its secrets to thunder
and ransom me home.

Beward oaks in laughter
know hemlock is lying
when she sings of defiance.
The sand words she is saying

will sift over and bury
while the pale moons I hate
seduce you in phases
through oceans of light.

And the wild trees shall sell me
for their safety from lightning
to sand that will flay me
for the next evening's planting.

They will fill my limp skin
with wild dreams from their root
and grow from my flesh
new handfuls of hate

till our ransom is wasted
and the morning speaks out
in a thin voice of wisdom
that loves me too late.

[1962]

Conversations In Crisis

I speak to you as a friend speaks
or a true lover
not out of friendship nor love
but for a clear meeting
of self upon self
in sight of our hearth
but without fire.

I cherish your words that ring
like late summer thunders
to sing without octave
and fade, having spoken the season.
But I hear the false heat of this voice
as it dries up the sides of your words
coaxing melodies from your tongue
and this curled music is treason.

Must I die in your fever—
or, as the flames wax, take cover
in your heart's culverts
crouched like a stranger
under scorched leaves of your other burnt loves
until the storm passes over?

[1962]

A Child Shall Lead

I have a child
whose feet are blind
on every road
but silence.

My boy has
lovely foolish lips
but cannot find
his way to sun

And I am grown
past knowledge.   [1962]

Now That I Am Forever With Child

How the days went
while you were blooming within me
I remember each upon each—
the swelling changed planes of my body
and how you first fluttered, then jumped
and I thought it was my heart.

How the days wound down
and the turning of winter
I recall, with you growing heavy
against the wind. I thought
now her hands
are formed, and her hair
has started to curl
now her teeth are done
now she sneezes.
Then the seed opened
I bore you one morning just before spring
My head rang like a fiery piston
my legs were towers between which
A new world was passing.

Since then
I can only distinguish

one thread within running hours
You, flowing through selves
toward You.

[1963]

What My Child Learns Of The Sea

What my child learns of the sea
of the summer thunders
of the riddles that hide in the curve of spring
she will learn in my twilights
and childlike
revise every autumn.

What my child learns
as her winters grow into time
has ripened in my own body
to enter her eyes with first light.

This is why
more than blood
or the milk I have given
one day a strange girl will step
to the back of a mirror
cutting my ropes
of sea and thunder and spring.
Of the way she will taste her autumns—
toast-brittle or warmer than sleep—
and the words she will use for winter
I stand already condemned.

[1963]

The Woman Thing

The hunters are back from beating the winter's face
in search of a challenge or task
in search of food
making fresh tracks for their children's hunger
they do not watch the sun
they cannot wear its heat for a sign
of triumph or freedom;
The hunters are treading heavily homeward

through snow that is marked
with their own bloody footprints.
emptyhanded, the hunters return
snow-maddened, sustained by their rages.

In the night after food they may seek
young girls for their amusement. But now
the hunters are coming
and the unbaked girls flee from their angers.
All this day I have craved
food for my child's hunger
Emptyhanded the hunters come shouting
injustices drip from their mouths
like stale snow melted in sunlight.

Meanwhile
the woman thing my mother taught me
bakes off its covering of snow
like a rising blackening sun.   [1964]

And What About The Children

Now we've made a child.
and the dire predictions
have changed into wild
grim
speculations;
still the negatives
are waiting
watching
and the relatives
keep right on
Touching . . .
              and how much curl
              is right for a girl?
But if it is said
at some future date
that my son's head
is on straight
he won't care
about his
hair

nor give a damn
whose wife
I am.

[1964]

Spring People

FOR JONNO

What anger in my hard-won bones
or heritage of water
makes me reject the april
and fear to walk upon the earth
in spring?

At springtime and evening
I recall how we came
like new thunder
beating the earth
leaving the taste of rain and sunset
all our hungers before us.
Away from the peace of half truths
and springtime passing unsaid
we came in the touch of fire
came to the sun
lay with a wild earth
until spent and knowing
we brought forth our young.

Now insolent aprils bedevil us—
earthy conceits—
to remind us that all else is forfeit
only our blood-hungry children
remember
what face we had
what startling eyes.

[1965]

Generation

How the young attempt and are broken
differs from age to age
We were brown free girls

love singing beneath our skin
sun in our hair in our eyes
sun our fortune
and the wind had made us golden
made us gay.

In a season of limited power
we wept out our promises
And these are the children we try now
for temptations that wear our face.
But who comes back from our latched cities of falsehood
to warn them the road to nowhere
is slippery with our blood
to warn them
they need not drink the river to get home
since we have purchased bridges
with our mothers' bloody gold;—
now we are more than kin
who come to share
not only blood
but the bloodiness of failure.

How the young are tempted and betrayed
into slaughter or conformity
is a turn of the mirror
time's question only.   [1966]

Bridge Through My Window

In curve scooped out and necklaced with light
burst pearls stream down my out-stretched arms to earth.
Oh bridge my sister bless me before I sleep
the wild air is lengthening
and I am tried beyond strength or bearing
over water.

Love, we are both shorelines
a left country
where time suffices
and the right land
where pearls roll into earth and spring up day.
Joined, our bodies have passage into one

without merging
as this slim necklace is anchored into night.

And while the we conspires
to make secret its two eyes
we search the other shore
for some crossing home.   [1966]

A Family Resemblance

My sister has my hair my mouth my eyes
and I presume her trustless.
When she was young and open to any fever
wearing gold like a veil of fortune on her face
she waited through each rain a dream of light.
But the sun came up
burning our eyes like crystal
bleaching the sky of promise and
my sister stood
Black, unblessed and unbelieving
shivering in the first cold show of love.

I saw her gold become an arch
where nightmare hunted
down the porches of restless night.
Now through echoes of denial
she walks a bleached side of reason.
Secret now
my sister never waits
nor mourns the gold that wandered from her bed.

My sister has my tongue
and all my flesh
unanswered
and I presume her trustless
as a stone.   [1966]

Rites Of Passage

TO MLR

Now rock the boat to a fare-thee-well.
Once we suffered dreaming
into the place where the children are playing
their child's games
where the children are hoping
knowledge survives if
unknowing
they follow the game
without winning.

Their fathers are dying
back to the freedom of wise children
playing at knowing
their fathers are dying
whose deaths will not free them
of growing from knowledge
of knowing
when the game becomes foolish
a dangerous pleading
for time of power.

Quick children
kiss us
we are growing
through dream.   [1968]

Rooming Houses Are Old Women

Rooming houses are old women
rocking dark windows into their whens
waiting incomplete circles
rocking
rent office to stoop to
community bathrooms to gas rings and
under-bed boxes of once useful garbage
city issued with a twice monthly check
and the young men next door
with their loud midnight parties

and fishy rings left in the bathtub
no longer arouse them
from midnight to mealtime no stops inbetween
light breaking to pass through jumbled up windows
and who was it who married the widow that Buzzie's son
      messed with?

To Welfare and insult from the slow shuffle
from dayswork to shopping bags
heavy with leftovers

Rooming houses
are old women waiting
searching
through darkening windows
the end or beginning of agony
old women seen through half-ajar doors
hoping
they are not waiting
but being
the entrance to somewhere
unknown and desired
but not new.

                             [1968]

On A Night Of The Full Moon

I

Out of my flesh that hungers
and my mouth that knows
comes the shape I am seeking
for reason.
The curve of your waiting body
fits my waiting hand
your breasts warm as sunlight
your lips quick as young birds
between your thighs the sweet
sharp taste of limes.

Thus I hold you
frank in my heart's eye
in my skin's knowing
as my fingers conceive your flesh

I feel your stomach
moving against me.

Before the moon wanes again
we shall come together.

II
And I would be the moon
spoken over your beckoning flesh
breaking against reservations
beaching thought
my hands at your high tide
over and under inside you
and the passing of hungers
attended, forgotten.

Darkly risen
the moon speaks
my eyes
judging your roundness
delightful.   [1968]

Hard Love Rock

Today I heard my heart screeching like a subway train
loudly enough to remind me it was still human
loudly enough to hurt
but telling me still
you were a ghost I had
better left in the cradle,
telling me still
that our tracks ran around
instead of straight out past the sewers
that I would have nothing for barter left
not even the print of love's grain
pressed into my flesh from our wooden cross
left splintered and shapeless
after the slaughter.

And when it was over
only pain.   [1968]

When The Saints Come Marching In

Plentiful sacrifice and believers in redemption
are all that is needed
so any day now
I expect some new religion
to rise up like tear gas
from the streets of New York
erupting like a rank pavement smell
released by the garbage-trucks'
baptismal drizzle.

The high priests have been ready and waiting
with their incense pans full of fire.
I do not know the rituals
the exhaltations
nor what name of the god
the survivors will worship
I only know she will be terrible
and very busy
and very old.   [1968]

Dreams Bite

I

Dreams bite.
The dreamer and his legends
arm at the edge of purpose.

Waking
I see the people of winter
put off their masks
to stain the earth red with blood
while
on the outer edges of sleep
the people of sun
are carving
their own children
into monuments
of war.

II

When I am absolute
at once
with the black earth
fire
I make
my nows
and power is spoken
peace
at rest and
hungry means never
or alone
I shall love
again ·

When I am obsolete.   [1968]

The Dozens

Nothing says that you must see me in the street
with us so close together at that red light
that a blind man could have smelled his grocer—
and nothing says that you must
say hello
as we pass in the street,
but we have known each other too well
in the dark
for this,
and it hurts me when you do not speak.

And no one you were with was quite so fine
that I won't remember this and
suffer you in turn and
in my own fashion which is certainly
not in the street.
For I can count on my telephone
ringing some evening and you
exploding into my room through the receiver
kissing and licking my ear. . . .

I hope you will learn your thing
at least

from some of those spiteful noseless
people who surround you
before the centipede in you
runs out of worlds

one for each foot.   [1968]

Fantasy And Conversation

Speckled frogs leap from my mouth
to drown in the coffee
between our wisdoms
and decision.

I could smile
and turn these frogs to pearls
speak of love, our making
our giving.
And if the spell works
shall I break down
or build what is broken
into a new house
shook with confusion

Shall I strike
before our magic
turns color?   [1968]

Martha

I

Martha this is a catalog of days
passing before you looked again.
Someday you will browse and order them
at will, or in your necessities.

I have taken a house at the Jersey shore
this summer. It is not my house.
Today the lightning bugs came.

On the first day you were dead.
With each breath the skin of your face moved
falling in like crumpled muslin.
We scraped together the smashed image of flesh
preparing a memory. No words.
No words.

On the eighth day
you startled the doctors
speaking from your deathplace
to reassure us that you were trying.

Martha these are replacement days
should you ever need them
given for those you once demanded and never found.
May this trip be rewarding;
no one can fault you again Martha
for answering necessity too well
may the gods who honor hard work
keep this second coming
free from that lack of choice
which hindered your first journey
to this Tarot house.

They said
no hope no dreaming
accept this case of flesh as evidence
of life without fire
and wrapped you in an electric blanket
kept ten degrees below life.
Fetal hands curled inward on the icy sheets
your bed was so cold
the bruises could not appear.

On the second day I knew you were alive
because the gray flesh of your face
suffered.

I love you and cannot feel you less than Martha
I love you and cannot split this shaved head
from Martha's pushy straightness
asking
in a smash of mixed symbols

How long must I wander here
in this final house of my father?

On the Solstice I was in Providence.
You know this town because you visited friends here.
It rained in Providence on the Solstice—
we passed through here twice
on route Six through Providence to the Cape
where we spent our second summer
trying for peace or equity, even.
It always seemed to be raining
by the time we got to Providence.
The Kirschenbaums live in Providence
and Blossom and Barry
and Frances. And Frances.
Martha I am in love again.
Listen, Frances, I said on the Solstice
our summer has started.
Today we are witches with enough energy
to move mountains back.
Think of Martha.

Back in my hideous city
I saw you today. Your hair has grown
and your armpits are scented
by some careful attendant.
Your *Testing testing testing*
explosive syllables warning me
of *The mountain has fallen into dung*—
no Martha remember remember Martha—
Warning
Dead flowers will not come to your bed again.
The sun has started south
our season is over.

Today you opened your eyes, giving
a blue-filmed history to your mangled words.
They help me understand
how you are teaching yourself to learn
again.

I need you need me
Je suis Martha I do not speak french kissing
Oh Wow. Black and . . . Black and . . . beautiful?

Black and becoming
somebody else maybe Erica maybe who sat
in the fourth row behind us in high school
but I never took French with you Martha
and who is this *Madame Erudite*
who is not me?

I found you today in a womb full of patients
blue-robed in various convalescences.
Your eyes are closed you are propped
into a wheelchair, cornered,
in a parody of resting.
The bright glue of tragedy plasters all eyes
to a television set in the opposite corner
where a man is dying
step by step
in the american ritual going.
Someone has covered you
for this first public appearance
in a hospital gown, a badge of your next step.
Evocative voices flow from the set
and the horror is thick
in this room full of broken and mending receptions.

But no one has told you what it's all about Martha
someone has shot another Kennedy
we are drifting closer to what you predicted
and your darkness is indeed speaking
Robert Kennedy is dying Martha
but not you not you not you
he has a bullet in his brain Martha
surgery was never considered for you
since there was no place to start
and no one intended to run you down on a highway
being driven home at 7:30 on a low summer evening
I gave a reading in Harlem that night
and who shall we try for this shaven head now
in the courts of heart Martha
where his murder is televised over and over
with residuals
they have caught the man who shot Robert Kennedy
who was another one of difficult journeys—
he has a bullet in his brain Martha
and much less of a chance than you.

On the first day of July you warned me again
the threads are broken
you darkened into explosive angers and
refused to open your eyes, humming interference
your thoughts are not over Martha
they are you and their task is
to remember Martha
we can help with the other
the mechanics of blood and bone
and you cut through the pain of my words
to warn me again
testing testing whoever passes
must tear out their hearing aids
for the duration.
I hear you explaining Neal
my husband whoever must give me a present
he has to give me
himself where I can find him for
where can he look at himself
in the mirror I am making
or over my bed where the window
is locked into battle with a wall?

Now I sit in New Jersey with lightning bugs and mosquitoes
typing and thinking of you.
Tonight you started seizures
which they say is a temporary relapse
but this lake is far away Martha
and I sit unquiet in New Jersey
thinking of you
I Ching the Book of Changes
says I am impertinent to ask of you obliquely
but I have no direct question
only need.
When I cast an oracle today
it spoke of the Abysmal again
which of all the hexagrams
is very difficult but very promising
in it water finds its own level, flowing
out from the lowest point.
And I cast another also that cautioned
the superior man to seek his strength
only in its own season.
Martha what did we learn from our brief season

when the summer grackles rang in my walls?
one and one is too late now
you journey through darkness alone
leafless I sit far from my present house
and the grackles' voices are dying

we shall love each other here if ever at all.

II

Yes foolish prejudice lies
I hear you Martha
that you would never harm my children
but you have forgotten their names
and that you are Elizabeth's godmother.
You offer me coral rings, watches
even your body
if I will help you sneak home.

No Martha my blood is not muddy my hands
are not dirty to touch
Martha I do not know your night nurse's name
even though she is Black
yes I did live in Brighton Beach once
which is almost Rockaway
one bitter winter
but not with your night nurse Martha
and yes I agree this is one hell
of a summer.

No you cannot walk yet Martha
and no the medicines you are given
to quiet your horrors
have not affected your brain
yes it is very hard to think but
it is getting easier and yes Martha
we have loved each other and yes I hope
we still can
no Martha I do not know if we shall ever
sleep in each other's arms again.

III

It is the middle of August and you are alive
to discomfort. You have been moved
into a utility room across the hall

from the critical ward because your screaming
disturbs the other patients
your bedside table has been moved also
which means you will be there for a while
a favorite now with the floor nurses
who put up a sign on the utility room door
I'M MARTHA HERE DO NOT FORGET ME
PLEASE KNOCK.

A golden attendant named Sukie
bathes you as you proposition her
she is very pretty and very gentle.
The frontal lobe of the brain governs inhibitions
the damage is after all slight
and they say the screaming will pass.

Your daughter Dorrie promises you
will be as good as new, Mama
who only wants to be *Bad as the old.*

I want some truth good hard truth
a sign of youth
we were all young once we had
a good thing going
now I'm making a plan
for a dead rabbit a rare rabbit.
I am dying goddammit dying am I
Dying?
Death is a word you can say now
pain is mortal
I am dying for god's sake won't someone please
get me a doctor PLEASE
your screams beat against our faces as you yell
begging relief from the blank cruelty
of a thousand nurses.
A moment of silence breaks
as you accumulate fresh sorrows
then through your pain-fired face
you slip me a wink

Martha Winked.

IV

Your face straightens into impatience
with the loads of shit you are handed
'You're doing just fine Martha what time is it Martha'
'What did you have for supper tonight Martha'
testing testing whoever passes for Martha
you weary of it.

All the people you must straighten out
pass your bedside in the utility room
bringing you cookies
and hoping
you will be kinder than they were.

Go away Mama and Bubie
for 30 years you made me believe
I was shit you shat out for the asking
but I'm not and you'd better believe it
right now would you kindly
stop rubbing my legs
and GET THE HELL OUT OF HERE.
Next week Bubie bring Teglach
your old favorite
and will you be kinder Martha
that we were to the shell the cocoon
out of which the you is emerging?

V

No one you were can come so close
to death without dying
into another Martha.
I await you
as we all await her
fearing her honesty
fearing
we may neither love nor dismiss
Martha with the dross burned away
fearing
condemnation from the essential.

You cannot get closer to death than this Martha
the nearest you've come to living yourself.

[June–August 1968]

Paperweight

Paper is neither kind nor cruel
merely white in its neutrality
I have for reality now
the brown bar of my arm
moving in broken rhythm
across this dead place.

All the poems I have ever written
are historical reviews of some now-absorbed country
a small judgment
hawking and coughing them up
I have ejected them not unlike children.
Now my throat is clear
and perhaps I shall speak again.

All the poems I have ever written
make a small book shaped like another me
called by yesterday's names
the shedding of a past in patched conceits
molted like snake skin—
a book of leavings.
I can do anything with them I wish
I can love them or hate them
use them for comfort or warmth
tissues or decoration
dolls or japanese baskets
blankets or spells.
I can use them for magic
lanterns or music
advice or small counsel
for napkins or past-times or
disposable diapers
I can make fire from them
or kindling
songs or paper chains

Or fold them all into a paper fan
with which to cool my husband's dinner.   [1969]

Poem For A Poet

I think of a coffin's quiet
when I sit in the world of my car
separate and observing
with the windows closed and washed clean
by the rain. I like to sit there
watching the other worlds pass. Yesterday evening
I sat in my car on Sheridan Square
flat and broke and a little bit damp
thinking about money and rain and how
the Village broads with their narrow hips
rolled like drunken shovels
down Christopher Street.

Then I saw you unmistakably
darting out from between a police car and
what used to be Atkin's all-night diner—
where we sat making bets the last time I saw you
on how many busts we could count through the plateglass
    window
in those last skinny hours before dawn
with our light worded-out but still burning
and the earlier evening's promise dregs in our coffee cups—
and I saw you dash out and turn left at the corner
your beard spiky with rain and refusing
shelter under your chin.

But I had thought you were dead Jarrell
struck down by a car at sunset on a North Carolina road
or were you the driver
tricked into a fatal swerve by some twilit shadow
or was that Frank O'Hara
or Conrad Kent Rivers
and you
the lonely spook in a Windy City motel
draped in the secrets of your convulsive death
all alone
all poets all loved and dying alone
that final death
less real than those deaths you lived
and for which I forgave you?

I watched you hurry down Fourth Street Jarrell
from the world of my car in the rain

remembering that Spring Festival Night
at Womens College in North Carolina
and wasn't that world a coffin's retreat
of spring whispers romance and rhetoric
Untouched
by the wind buffeting up the road from Greensboro
and nobody mentioned the Black Revolution
or Sit-Ins or Freedom Rides or SNCC
or cattle-prods in Jackson Mississippi—
where I was to find myself how many years later:

You were mistaken that night and I told you
in a letter beginning—Dear Jarrell
if you sit in one place long enough
the whole world will pass you by . . .
you were wrong when you said I took
living too seriously
meaning you were afraid I might take you
too seriously
you shouldn't have worried because
I dug you too much
to put you down
but I never took you at all
except as a good piece of my first journey south
except as I take you now
gladly and separate at a distance
and wondering
as I have so often
how come being so cool
you weren't also a little bit
black.

And also why you have returned
to this dying city
and what piece of me is it then
buried down there in North Carolina.   [1970]

Story Books On A Kitchen Table

Out of her womb of pain my mother spat me
into her ill-fitting harness of despair
into her deceits
where anger re-conceived me
piercing my eyes like arrows
pointed by her nightmare
of who I was not
becoming.

Going away
she left in her place
iron maidens to protect me
and for my food
the wrinkled milk of legend
where I wandered through the lonely rooms of afternoon
wrapped in nightmares
from the Orange and Red and Yellow
Purple and Blue and Green
Fairy Books
where white witches ruled
over the empty kitchen table
and never wept
or offered gold
nor any kind enchantment
for the vanished mother
of a Black girl.   [1970]

From **From a Land Where**

Other People Live

Equinox

My daughter marks the day that spring begins.
I cannot celebrate spring without remembering
how the bodies of unborn children
bake in their mothers flesh like ovens
consecrated to the flame that eats them
lit by mobiloil and easternstandard
Unborn children in their blasted mothers
floating like small monuments
in an ocean of oil.

The year my daughter was born
DuBois died in Accra while I
marched into Washington
to a death knell of dreaming
which 250,000 others mistook for a hope
believing only Birmingham's black children
were being pounded into mortar in churches
that year
some of us still thought
Vietnam was a suburb of Korea.

Then John Kennedy fell off the roof
of Southeast Asia
and shortly afterward my whole house burned down
with nobody in it
and on the following sunday my borrowed radio announced
that Malcolm was shot dead
and I ran to reread
all that he had written
because death was becoming such an excellent measure
of prophecy
As I read his words the dark mangled children
came streaming out of the atlas
Hanoi Angola Guinea-Bissau Mozambique Pnom-Phen
merged into Bedford-Stuyvesant and Hazelhurst Mississippi
haunting my New York tenement that terribly bright
     summer
while Detroit and Watts and San Francisco were burning
I lay awake in stifling Broadway nights afraid
for whoever was growing in my belly
and suppose it started earlier than planned
who would I trust to take care that my daughter

did not eat poisoned roaches
when I was gone?

If she did, it doesn't matter
because I never knew it.
Today both children came home from school
talking about spring and peace
and I wonder if they will ever know it
I want to tell them we have no right to spring
because our sisters and brothers are burning
because every year the oil grows thicker
and even the earth is crying
because black is beautiful but currently
going out of style
that we must be very strong
and love each other
in order to go on living.   [1969]

The Seventh Sense

Women
who build nations
learn
to love
men
who build nations
learn
to love
children
building sand castles
by the rising sea.   [1969]

Change Of Season

Am I to be cursed forever with becoming
somebody else on the way to myself?

Walking backward I fall
into summers behind me
salt with wanting

lovers or friends a job wider shoes
a cool drink
freshness something to bite into
a place to hide out of the rain
out of the shifting melange of seasons
where the cruel boys I chased
and their skinny dodgeball sisters
flamed and died in becoming
the brown autumn
left in search of who tore the streamers down
at graduation christmas my wedding day
and as winter wore out the babies came
angry effort and reward
in their appointed seasons
my babies tore out of me
like poems
after
I slept and woke to the thought
that promise had come again
this time more sure than the dream of being
sweet sixteen and somebody else
walking five miles through the august city
with a free dog
thinking
now we will be the allamerican family
we had just gotten a telephone
and the next day my sister cut his leash on Broadway
that dog of my childhood bays at the new moon
as I reach into time up to my elbows
extracting the taste and the sharp smell
of my first lover's neck
rough as the skin of a brown pear ripening
I was so terribly sure I would come forever to april
with my first love who died on a sunday morning
poisoned and wondering
was summer ever coming.

As I face an ocean of seasons they start
to separate into distinct and particular faces
listening to the cover beginning to crack open
and whether or not the fruit is worth waiting
thistles and arrows and apples are blooming
the individual beautiful faces are smiling and moving
even the pavement begins to flow into new concretions
the eighth day is coming

I have paid dearly in time for love I hoarded
unseen
summer goes into my words
and comes out reason.   [1969]

For Each Of You

Be who you are and will be
learn to cherish
that boisterous Black Angel that drives you
up one day and down another
protecting the place where your power rises
running like hot blood
from the same source
as your pain.

When you are hungry
learn to eat
whatever sustains you
until morning
but do not be misled by details
simply because you live them.

Do not let your head deny
your hands
any memory of what passes through them
nor your eyes
nor your heart
everything can be used
except what is wasteful
(you will need
to remember this when you are accused of destruction).
Even when they are dangerous
examine the heart of those machines
which you hate
before you discard them
but do not mourn the lack of their power
lest you be condemned
to relive them.

If you do not learn to hate
you will never be lonely

enough
to love easily
nor will you always be brave
although it does not grow any easier
Do not pretend to convenient beliefs
even when they are righteous
you will never be able to defend your city
while shouting

Remember
our sun
is not the most noteworthy star
only the nearest

Respect whatever pain you bring back
from your dreaming
but do not look for new gods
in the sea
nor in any part of a rainbow

Each time you love
love as deeply
as if it were
forever
only nothing is
eternal.

Speak proudly to your children
where ever you may find them
tell them
you are the offspring of slaves
and your mother was
a princess
in darkness.   [1970]

Good Mirrors Are Not Cheap

It is a waste of time hating a mirror
or its reflection
instead of stopping the hand
that makes glass with distortions
slight enough to pass

unnoticed
until one day you peer
into your face
under a merciless white light
and the fault in a mirror slaps back
becoming
what you think
is the shape of your error
and if I am beside that self
you destroy me
or if you can see
the mirror is lying
you shatter the glass
choosing another blindness
and slashed helpless hands.

Because at the same time
down the street
a glassmaker is grinning
turning out new mirrors that lie
selling us
new clowns
at cut rate.   [1970]

As I Grow Up Again

A little boy wears my mistakes
like a favorite pair of shorts
outgrown
at six
my favorite excuse was morning
and I remember that I hated
springs change.

At play within my childhood
my son works hard
learning
the doors that do not open easily
and which clocks will not work
he toys with anger like a young cat
testing its edges
slashing through the discarded box

where I laid my childish dreams to rest
and brought him brown and wriggling
to his own house.

He learns there through my error
winning with secrets
I do not need to know.   [1970]

New Year's Day

The day feels put together hastily
like a gift for grateful beggars
being better than no time at all
but the bells are ringing
in cities I have never visited
and my name is printed over doorways
I have never seen
While extracting a bone
or whatever is tender or fruitful
from the core of indifferent days
I have forgotten
the touch of sun
cutting through uncommitted mornings
The night is full of messages
I cannot read
I am too busy forgetting
air like fur on my tongue
and these tears
which do not come from sadness
but from grit in a sometimes wind

Rain falls like tar on my skin
my son picks up a chicken heart at dinner
asking
does this thing love?
Deft unmalicious fingers of ghosts
pluck over my dreaming
hiding whatever it is of sorrow
that would profit me
I am deliberate
and afraid
of nothing.   [1970]

Neighbors

FOR D.D.

We made strong poems for each other
exchanging formulas for our own particular magic
all the time pretending
we were not really witches
and each time we would miss
some small ingredient
that one last detail
that could make the spell work
Each one of us
too busy
hearing our other voices
the sound of our own guards
calling the watch at midnight
assuring us
we were still safely asleep
so when it came time to practice
what we had learned
one grain was always missing
one word unsaid
so the pot did not boil
the sweet milk would curdle
or the bright wound went on bleeding
and each of us would go back
to her own particular magic
confirmed
believing
she was always alone
believing
the other was always
lying
in wait.   [1970]

Love, Maybe

Always
in the middle
of our bloodiest battles
you lay down your arms
like flowering mines

to conqueror me home.   [1970]

Conclusion

Passing men in the street who are dead
becomes a common occurrence
but loving one of them
is no solution.
I believe in love as I believe in our children
but I was born Black and without illusion
and my vision
which differs from yours
is clear
although sometimes restricted.

I have watched you at midnight
moving through casual sleep
wishing I could afford the non-desperate dreams
that stir you
to wither and fade into partial solutions.
Your nights are wintery long and very young
full of symbols of purity and forgiveness
and a meek jesus that rides through your cities
on a barren ass whose braying
does not include a future tense.

But I wear my nights as I wear my life
and my dying
absolute and unforgiven
suggests of compromise and decision
fossilized by fierce midsummer sun
and when I dream
I move through a Black land

where the future
glows eternal and green
but where the symbols for now
are bloody and unrelenting
rooms
where confused children
with wooden stumps for fingers
play at war
who cannot pick up their marbles
and run away home
whenever a nightmare threatens.

[1970]

The Winds of Orisha

I

This land will not always be foreign.
How many of its women ache to bear their stories
robust and screaming like the earth erupting grain
or thrash in padded chains mute as bottles
hands fluttering traces of resistance
on the backs of once lovers
half the truth
knocking in the brain like an angry steampipe
how many
long to work or split open
so bodies venting into silence
can plan the next move?

Tiresias too 500 years they say to progress into woman
growing smaller and darker and more powerful
until nut-like, she went to sleep in a bottle
Tiresias took 500 years to grow into woman
so do not despair of your sons.

II

Impatient legends speak through my flesh
changing this earths formation
spreading
I will become myself
an incantation
dark raucous many-shaped characters
leaping back and forth across bland pages

and Mother Yemanja raises her breasts to begin my labor
near water
the beautiful Oshun and I lie down together
in the heat of her body truth my voice comes stronger
Shango will be my brother roaring out of the sea
earth shakes our darkness swelling into each other
warning winds will announce us living
as Oya, Oya my sister my daughter
destroys the crust of the tidy beaches
and Eshu's black laughter turns up the neat sleeping sand.

III

The heart of this country's tradition is its wheat men
dying for money
dying for water for markets for power
over all people's children
they sit in their chains on their dry earth
before nightfall
telling tales as they wait for their time
of completion
hoping the young ones can hear them
earth-shaking fears wreathe their blank weary faces
most of them have spent their lives and their wives
in labor
most of them have never seen beaches
but as Oya my sister moves out of the mouths
of their sons and daughters against them
I will swell up from the pages of their daily heralds
leaping out of the almanacs
instead of an answer to their search for rain they will read me
the dark cloud
meaning something entire
and different.

When the winds of Orisha blow
even the roots of grass
quicken.   [1970]

Who Said It Was Simple

There are so many roots to the tree of anger
that sometimes the branches shatter
before they bear.

Sitting in Nedicks
the women rally before they march
discussing the problematic girls
they hire to make them free.
An almost white counterman passes
a waiting brother to serve them first
and the ladies neither notice nor reject
the slighter pleasures of their slavery.
But I who am bound by my mirror
as well as my bed
see causes in color
as well as sex

and sit here wondering
which me will survive
all these liberations.   [1970]

The Day They Eulogized Mahalia

The day they eulogized Mahalia
the echoes of her big voice were stilled
and the mourners found her
singing out from their sisters mouths
from their mothers toughness
from the funky dust in the corners
of sunday church pews
sweet and dry and simple
and that hated sunday morning fussed over feeling
the songs
singing out from their mothers toughness
would never threaten the lord's retribution
any more.

Now she was safe
acceptable
that big Mahalia
Chicago turned all out
to show her that they cared
but her eyes were closed
And although Mahalia loved our music
nobody sang her favorite song
and while we talked about
what a hard life she had known

and wasn't it too bad Sister Mahalia
didn't have it easier
earlier
Six Black children
burned to death in a day care center
on the South Side
kept in a condemned house
for lack of funds
firemen found their bodies
like huddled lumps of charcoal
with silent mouths and eyes wide open.
Small and without song
six black children found a voice in flame
the day the city eulogized Mahalia.   [1971]

Progress Report

These days
when you do say hello I am never sure
if you are being saucy or experimental or
merely protecting some new position.
Sometimes you gurgle while asleep
and I know tender places still intrigue you.
Now
when you question me on love
shall I recommend a dictionary
or myself?

You are the child of wind and ravens I created
always my daughter
I cannot recognize
the currents where you swim and dart
through my loving
upstream to your final place of birth
but you never tire of hearing
how I crept out of my mother's house
at dawn, with an olive suitcase
crammed with books and fraudulent letters
and an unplayed guitar.

Sometimes I see myself flash through your eyes
in a moment
caught between history and obedience

that moment grows each day
before you comply
as, when did washing dishes
change from privilege to chore?
I watch the hollows deepen above your hips
and wonder if I have taught you Black enough
until I see
all kinds of loving still intrigue you
as you grow more and more
dark rude and tender
and unfraid.

What you took for granted once
you now refuse to take at all
even I
knock before I enter
the shoals of furious choices
not my own
that flood through your secret reading
nightly, under cover.
I have not yet seen you, but
I hear the pages rustle
from behind closed doors.   [1971]

Black Mother Woman

I cannot recall you gentle
yet through your heavy love
I have become
an image of your once delicate flesh
split with deceitful longings.

When strangers come and compliment me
your aged spirit takes a bow
jingling with pride
but once you hid that secret
in the center of furies
hanging me
with deep breasts and wiry hair
with your own split flesh
and long suffering eyes
buried in myths of little worth.

But I have peeled away your anger
down to the core of love
and look mother
I Am
a dark temple where your true spirit rises
beautiful
and tough as chestnut
stanchion against your nightmare of weakness
and if my eyes conceal
a squadron of conflicting rebellions
I learned from you
to define myself
through your denials.   [1971]

Teacher

I make my children promises in wintery afternoons
like lunchtime stories
when my feet hurt from talking too much
and not enough movement except in my own
worn down at the heel shoes
except in the little circle of broken down light
I am trapped in
the intensities of my own (our) situation
where what we need and do not have
deadens us
and promises sound like destruction
white snowflakes clog the passages
drifting through the halls and corridors
while I tell stories with no ending
at lunchtime
the children's faces bear uneasy smiles
like a heavy question
I provide food with a frightening efficiency
the talk is free/dom meaning state
condition of being
We are elementary forces colliding in free fall.

And who will say I made promises
better kept in confusion
than time
grown tall and straight in a season of snow

in a harsh time of the sun that withers
who will say as they build
ice castles at noon
living the promises I made
these children
who will say
look—we have laid out the new cities
with more love than our dreams
Who will hear
freedom's bell deaden
in the clang of the gates of the prisons
where snow-men melt into darkness
unforgiven and so remembered
while the hot noon speaks in a fiery voice?

How we romped through so many winters
made snowballs play at war
rubbing snow against our brown faces
and they tingled and grew bright
in the winter sun
instead of chocolate we rolled snow
over our tongues
until it melted like sugar
burning the cracks in our lips
and we shook our numbed fingers
all the way home
remembering
summer was coming.

As the promises I make children
sprout like wheat from an early spring's wager
who will hear freedom
ring in the chains of promise
who will forget the curse
of the outsider
who will not recognize our season
as free
who will say
Promise corrupts
what it does not invent.   [1971]

Generation II

A Black girl
going
into the woman
her mother
desired
and prayed for
walks alone
and afraid
of both their angers.   [1971]

Relevant Is
Different Points On The Circle

TO BWC

History
bless me with my children's growing rebellion
with love in another tongue
teach me what my pride will not savor
like the fabled memory of elephants
I have loved them and watched over them
as the bird forgets but the trap doesn't
and I shall be buried with the bones of an eagle
with a fierce detachment
and legends of the slain buffalo.

This is a country where other people live.

When agate replaces dead wood
slowly the opal and bone become one.
A phoenix named Angela
nests in my children's brain
already
growing herds of bison unnoticed
are being hunted down the federal canyons
of Yellowstone Park.   [1971]

Dear Toni
Instead Of A Letter Of Congratulation
Upon Your Book And Your Daughter
Whom You Say You Are Raising To Be
A Correct Little Sister

I can see your daughter walking down streets of love
in revelation;
but raising her up to be a correct little sister
is doing your mama's job all over again.
And who did you make on the edge of Harlem's winter
hard and black
while the inside was undetermined
swirls of color and need
shifting, remembering
were you making another self to rediscover
in a new house and a new name
in a new place next to a river of blood
or were you putting the past together
pooling everything learned
into a new and continuous woman
divorced
from the old shit we share
and shared and sharing need not share again?

I see your square delicate jawbone
the mark of a Taurus (or Leo) as well as the ease
with which you deal with your pretensions.
I dig your going and becoming
the lessons you teach your daughter
our history
for I am your sister corrected and
already raised up
our daughters will explore the old countries
as curious visitors to our season
using their own myths to keep themselves sharp.

I have known you over and over again
as I've lived throughout this city
taking it in storm and morning strolls
through Astor Place and under the Canal Street Bridge
The Washington Arch like a stone raised to despair
and Riverside Drive too close to the dangerous predawn

waters and 129th Street between Lenox and Seventh
burning my blood but not black enough
and threatening to become home.

I first saw you behind a caseworker's notebook
defying upper Madison Avenue and my roommate's
        concern
the ghost of Maine lobsterpots trailing behind you
and I followed you into east fourth street and out
through Bellevue's side entrance one night
into the respectable vineyards of Yeshivas intellectual
        gloom
and there I lost you between the books and the games
until I rose again out of Jackson Mississippi
to find you in an office down the hall from mine
calmly studying term papers like maps
marking off stations
on our trip through the heights of Convent Avenue
teaching english our children citycollege
softer and tougher and more direct
and putting your feet up on a desk you say Hi
I'm going to have a baby so now I can really indulge
        myself.
Through that slim appraisal of your world
I felt you
grinning and plucky and a little bit scared
perhaps of the madness past that had relieved you
through your brittle young will of iron
into the fire of whip steel.

I have a daughter also
who does not remind me of you
but she too has deep aquatic eyes that are burning and
        curious.
As she moves through taboos
whirling myths like gay hoops over her head
I know beyond fear and history
that our teaching means keeping trust
with less and less correctness
only with ourselves—
History may alter
old pretenses and victories
but not the pain my sister never the pain.

In my daughter's name
I bless your child with the mother she has
with a future of warriors and growing fire.
But with tenderness also,
for we are landscapes, Toni,
printed upon them as surely
as water etches feather on stone.
Our girls will grow into their own
Black Women
finding their own contradictions
that they will come to love
as I love you.   [September 1971]

Prologue

Haunted by poems beginning with I
seek out those whom I love who are deaf
to whatever does not destroy
or curse the old ways that did not serve us
while history falters and our poets are dying
choked into silence by icy distinction
their death rattles blind curses
and I hear even my own voice becoming
a pale strident whisper
At night sleep locks me into an echoless coffin
sometimes at noon I dream
there is nothing to fear
now standing up in the light of my father sun
without shadow
I speak without concern for the accusations
that I am too much or too little woman
that I am too black or too white
or too much myself
and through my lips come the voices
of the ghosts of our ancestors
living and moving among us
Here my heart's voice as it darkens
pulling old rhythms out of the earth
that will receive this piece of me
and a piece of each one of you
when our part in history quickens again
and is over:

Hear
the old ways are going away
and coming back pretending change
masked as denunciation and lament
masked as a choice
between eager mirrors that blur and distort
us in easy definitions
until our image
shatters along its fault
while the other half of that choice
speaks to our hidden fears with a promise
that our eyes need not seek any truer shape—
a face at high noon particular and unadorned—
for we have learned to fear
the light from clear water might destroy us
with reflected emptiness or a face without tongue
with no love or with terrible penalties
for any difference
and even as I speak remembered pain is moving
shadows over my face, my own voice fades and
my brothers and sisters are leaving;

Yet when I was a child
whatever my mother thought would mean survival
made her try to beat me whiter every day
and even now the color of her bleached ambition
still forks throughout my words
but I survived
and didn't I survive confirmed
to teach my children where her errors lay
etched across their faces between the kisses
that she pinned me with asleep
and my mother beating me
as white as snow melts in the sunlight
loving me into her bloods black bone—
the home of all her secret hopes and fears
and my dead father whose great hands
weakened in my judgment
whose image broke inside of me
beneath the weight of failure
helps me to know who I am not
for weak or mistaken
my father loved me alive
to grow and hate him

and now his grave voice joins hers
within my words rising and falling
are my sisters and brothers listening?

The children remain
like blades of grass over the earth and
all the children are singing
louder than mourning
all their different voices sound like a raucous question
but they do not fear blank and empty mirrors
they have seen their faces defined in a hydrants puddle
before the rainbows of oil obscured them.

The time of lamentation and curses is passing.

My mother survives now
through more than chance or token.
Although she will read what I write with embarrassment
or anger
and a small understanding
my children do not need to relive my past
in strength nor in confusion
nor care that their holy fires
may destroy
more than my failures

Somewhere in the landscape past noon
I shall leave a dark print
of the me that I am
and who I am not
etched in a shadow of angry and remembered loving
and their ghosts will move
whispering through them
with me none the wiser
for they will have buried me
either in shame
or in peace.

And the grasses will still be
Singing.   [November 1971]

Moving Out Or
The End Of Cooperative Living

I am so glad to be moving
away from this prison for black and white faces
assaulting each other with our joint oppression
competing for who pays the highest price for this privilege
I am so glad I am moving
technicolored complaints aimed at my head
mash up on my door like mosquitoes
sweep like empty ladles through the lobby of my eyes
each time my lips move sideways
the smile shatters
on the in-thing that races
dictator through our hallways
on concrete faces on soul compactors
on the rhetoric of incinerators and plastic drapes
for the boiler room
on legends of broken elevators
blowing my morning cool
avoiding me in the corridors
dropping their load on my face down 24 stories
of lives in a spectrumed madhouse
pavillion of gnats and nightmare remembering
once we all saved like beggars
to buy our way into this castle
of fantasy and forever now
I am so glad to be moving.

Last month a tenant was asked to leave
because someone saw him
wandering one morning up and down the tenth floor
with no clothes on
having locked himself out the night before
with the garbage
he could not fit into the incinerator
but it made no difference
the floor captain cut the leads to his cable TV
and he left covered in tangled wires of shame
his apartment was reconsecrated by a fumigator
I am so glad I am moving

Although workmen will descend at $100 an hour
to scrape my breath from the walls

to refinish the air and the floors with their eyes
and charge me the exact amount
of whatever I have coming back to me
called equity
I am so glad to be moving
from the noise of psychic footsteps
beating a tune that is not my own
louder than any other sound in the neighborhood
except the blasting that goes on all day and all night
from the city's new toilet being built
outside the main entrance
from the spirits who live in the locks
of the other seven doors
bellowing secrets of living hells revealed
but not shared
for everybody's midnights know what the walls hide
our toilets are made of glass
wired for sound

24 stories
full of tears flushing at midnight
our only community room
children set their clocks to listen at the tissue walls
gazing upward from their stools
from one flight to another
catching the neighbors in private struggle
next morning it will all be discussed
at length in the elevators
with no secrets left
I am so glad to be moving
no more coming home at night to dream
of caged puppies
grinding their teeth into cartoonlike faces
that half plead and half snicker
then fold under and vanish
back into snarling strangers
I am so glad I am moving.

But when this grim house goes
slipping into the sewer prepared for it
then this whole city can read
its own obituary
written on the broken record of dreams
of ordinary people

who wanted what they could not get
and so pretended to be someone else
ordinary people having
what they never learned to want
themselves
and so becoming
pretension concretized.   [1972]

Moving In

*"It is the worst of luck to bring into a new house from
the old bread salt or broomstick."*

> Salt Bread and Broom
> be still.
> I leave you guardian
> against gone places
> I have loved
> your loss
> a green promise
> making new
> Salt
> Bread
> and Broom
> remove me from the was
> I still am
> to now
> becoming
> here this house
> forever blessed.   [1972]

Movement Song

I have studied the tight curls on the back of your neck
moving away from me
beyond anger or failure
your face in the evening schools of longing
through mornings of wish and ripen
we were always saying goodbye
in the blood in the bone over coffee
before dashing for elevators going

in opposite directions
without goodbyes.

Do not remember me as a bridge nor a roof
as the maker of legends
nor as a trap
door to that world
where black and white clericals
hang on the edge of beauty in five o'clock elevators
twitching their shoulders to avoid other flesh
and now
there is someone to speak for them
moving away from me into tomorrows
morning of wish and ripen
your goodbye is a promise of lightning
in the last angels hand
unwelcome and warning
the sands have run out against us
we were rewarded by journeys
away from each other
into desire
into mornings alone
where excuse and endurance mingle
conceiving decision.

Do not remember me
as disaster
nor as the keeper of secrets
I am the fellow rider in the cattle cars
watching
you move
slowly out of my bed
saying we cannot waste time
only ourselves.   [1972]

From **New York Head Shop
and Museum**

Mentor

Scaling your words like crags I found
silence
speaking in amouthful of sun
and I say you are young
for your lips are not stone
to the rain's fall
I say you are lovely to speak
in a mouthful of sun
nor does summer await you.

I see the midnight
heavy as windows sealed against fire
and the tears
coiled like snakes in your eyes
I see your forehead like snow
and the names of the so many winters
your fingers play over
plucking out rays of light
to anoint me home;

Yet I say you are young
and your lips are not stone
to be weathered
rather a song
learned when my aprils were fallow.
I sing this for beacon now
lighting us home
each to our separate house.   [1959]

The Fallen

*M'lord, the stars no longer concern themselves with
you, Druon*

Bright uncanny music was beating through the room
We had come
afraid
to seek some long range
and less threatening death
for us
but the coffee fouled with memory

and I spoke through a mouth
of unshed tears.
Your wild hair curled about your eyes
like commas
in a poem I could not read.
Our words fell
crumpled empty circles
and the beating rain outside
told far more truth.   [1959]

Revolution Is One Form
Of Social Change

When the man is busy
making niggers
it doesn't matter
much
what shade
you are.

If he runs out of one
particular color
he can always switch
to size
and when he's finished
off the big ones
he'll just change
to sex
which is
after all
where it all began.   [1968]

The American Cancer Society Or
There Is More Than One Way
To Skin a Coon

Of all the ways in which this country
Prints its death upon me
Selling me cigarettes is one of the most certain.

Yet every day I watch my son digging
ConEdison GeneralMotors GarbageDisposal
Out of his nose as he watches a 3 second spot
On How To Stop Smoking
And it makes me sick to my stomach.
For it is not by cigarettes
That you intend to destroy my children.

Not even by the cold white light of moon-walks
While half the boys I knew
Are doomed to quicker trips by a different capsule;
No, american cancer destroys
By seductive and reluctant admission
For instance
Black women no longer give birth through our ears
and therefore have A Monthly Need For Iron:
For instance
Our Pearly teeth are *not* racially insured
And therefore must be Gleemed For Fewer Cavities:
For instance
Even though the astronauts are white
Perhaps Black People *can* develop
Some of those human attributes
Requiring
Dried dog food frozen coffee instant oatmeal
Depilatories deodorants detergents
And other assorted plastic.

And this is the surest sign I know
That the american cancer society is dying—
It has started to dump its symbols onto Black People
A convincing proof those symbols are now useless
And far more lethal than emphysema.   [1969]

A Sewerplant Grows In Harlem Or
I'm a Stranger Here Myself
When Does The Next Swan Leave

How is the word made flesh made steel made shit
by ramming it into No Exit like a homemade bomb
until it explodes
smearing itself

made real
against our already filthy windows
or by flushing it out in a verbal fountain?
Meanwhile the editorial They—
who are no less powerful—
prepare to smother the actual Us
with a processed flow of all our shit
non-verbal.

Have you ever risen in the night
bursting with knowledge and the world
dissolves toward any listening ear
into which you can pour
whatever it was you knew
before waking
Only to find all ears asleep
or drugged perhaps by a dream of words
because as you scream into them over and over
nothing stirs
and the mind you have reached is not a working mind
please hang up and die again? The mind
you have reached is not a working mind
Please hang up
And die again.

Talking to some people is like talking to a toilet.   [1969]

Cables To Rage Or
I've Been Talking On This Street Corner
A Hell Of A Long Time

This is how I came to be loved
by loving myself loveless.

One day I slipped in the snowy gutter of Brighton Beach
and the booted feet passing
me by on the curb squished my laundry ticket
into the slush and I thought oh fuck it now
I'll never get my clean sheet and I cried bitter tears
into the snow under my cheek in that gutter in Brighton Beach
Brooklyn where I was living because it was cheap

In a furnished room with cooking privileges
and there was an old thrown-away mama who lived down the hall
a yente who sat all day long in our common kitchen
weeping because her children made her live with a schwartze
and while she wept she drank up all my Cream Soda
every day before I came home.
Then she sat and watched me watching my chicken feet stewing
on Fridays when I got paid
and she taught me to boil old corn in the husk
to make it taste green and fresh.
There were not many pleasures in that winter
and I loved Cream Soda
there were not many people in that winter
and I came to hate that old woman.
The winter I got fat on stale corn on the cob
and chicken foot stew and the day before Christmas
having no presents to wrap
I poured two ounces of Nux Vomica into a bottle of Cream Soda
and listened to the old lady puke all night long.

When spring came I crossed the river again
moving up in the world six and a half stories
and one day on the corner of eighth street across from Wanamakers
which had burned down while I was away in Brooklyn—
where I caught the bus for work every day
a bus driver slowed down at the bus stop one morning—
I was late it was raining and my jacket was soaked—
and then speeded past without stopping when he saw my face.

I have been given other doses of truth—
that particular form of annihilation—
shot through by the cold eye of the way things are baby
and left for dead on a hundred streets of this city
but oh that captain marvel glance
brushing up against my skull like a steel bar
in passing
and my heart withered sheets in the gutter
passing passing
booted feet and bus drivers
and old yentes in Brighton Beach kitchens

SHIT! said the king and the whole court strained
passing

me out as an ill-tempered wind
lashing around the corner
of 125th Street and Lenox.   [1969]

Release Time

I came to their white
terror first
the nuns with their ghostly motives
hidden in black
motionless
yet always upon us before we sinned
always knowing
and smiling
sadly.

Was it the neat sample loaves
of stale Silvercup bread
and lukewarm milk
doled out in the chalky afternoons
or the threat of public school always
hanging over us
that made me want to believe
the slight face of magic
marooned in an ocean of black
shaping the words by which I learned

to pray to almighty god to
blessed michael the archangel
defend us in battle be our protection
against the wickedness and snares of
the devil who comes
white robed
to our daily crucifixions
restrain him oh lord we beseech and implore
you
who shall not hear us
pray again
except to seek in ourselves
what is human to sustain us
and less terror
for our children.   [1969]

Ballad From Childhood

Mommy mommy come and see
what the strawmen left for me
in our land of ice and house of snow
I have found a seed to grow
Mommy may I plant a tree?

What the eyes don't see the heart don't hurt.

But mommy look the seed has wings
my tree might call a bird that sings . . .
true, the strawmen left no spade no earth
and ice will not bring my seed to birth—
but what if I dig beneath these things?

Watch the birds forget but the trap doesn't.

Please mommy do not beat me so!
yes I will learn to love the snow!
yes I want neither seed nor tree!
yes ice is quite enough for me!
who knows what trouble-leaves might grow!

I don't fatten frogs to feed snakes.   [1969]

New York City

I

How do you spell change like frayed slogan underwear
with the emptied can of yesterdays' meanings
with yesterday's names?
And what does the we-bird see with
who has lost its I's?

There is nothing beautiful left in the streets of this city.
I have come to believe in death and renewal by fire.
Past questioning the necessities of blood
or why it must be mine or my children's time
that will see the grim city quake to be reborn perhaps
blackened again but this time with a sense of purpose;
tired of the past tense forever, of assertion and repetition
of the ego-trips through an incomplete self

where two years ago proud rang for promise but now
it is time for fruit and all the agonies are barren—
only the children are growing:

And how else can the self become whole
save by making self into its own new religion?
Yet I am bound like an old lover—a true believer—
to this city's death by accretion and slow ritual,
and I submit to its penance for a trial
as new steel is tried
I submit my children also to its agonies
and they are not the city's past lovers. But I submit them
to the harshness and growing cold to the brutalizations
which if survived
will teach them strength
or an understanding of how strength is gotten
and will not be forgotten: It will be their city then:
I submit them
loving them above all others save myself
to the fire to the rage to the ritual sacrifications
to be tried as new steel is tried;
and in its wasting the city shall try them
as the blood-splash of a royal victim
tries the hand of the destroyer.

II

I hide behind tenements and subways in fluorescent alleys
watching as flames walk the streets of an empire's altar
rage through the veins of a sacrificial stenchpot
smeared on the east shore of a continent's insanity
conceived in the psychic twilight of murderers and pilgrims
rank with money and nightmare and too many useless people
who will not move over nor die, who cannot bend
even before the winds of their own preservation
even under the weight of their own hates
Who cannot amend nor conceive nor even learn to share
their own visions
who bomb my children into mortar in churches
and work plastic offal and metal and the flesh of their enemies
into subway rush-hour temples where obscene priests
finger and worship each other in secret
They think they are praying when they squat
to shit money-pebbles shaped like their parents' brains—
who exist to go into dust to exist again

grosser and more swollen and without ever relinquishing
space or breath or energy from their private hoard.

I do not need to make war nor peace
with these prancing and murderous deacons
who refuse to recognize their role in this covenant we live upon
and so have come to fear and despise even their own children;
but I condemn myself, and my loves
past and present
and the blessed enthusiasms of all my children
to this city
without reason or future
without hope
to be tried as the new steel is tried
before trusted to slaughter.

I walk down the withering limbs of my last discarded house
and there is nothing worth salvage left in this city
but the faint reedy voices like echoes
of once beautiful children.   [1971]

To The Girl Who Lives In A Tree

A letter in my mailbox says you've made it
to Honduras and I wonder what is the color
of the wood you are chopping now.

When you left this city I wept for a year
down 14th Street across the Taconic Parkway
through the shingled birdcotes along Riverside Drive
and I was glad because in your going
you left me a new country
where Riverside Drive became an embattlement
that even dynamite could not blast free
where making both love and war became less inconsistent
and as my tears watered morning I became
my own place to fathom
While part of me follows you still thru the woods of Oregon
splitting dead wood with a rusty axe
acting out the nightmares of your mothers
creamy skin soot-covered from communal fires
where you provide and labor to discipline your dreams

whose symbols are immortalized in lies of history
told like fairy tales called power
behind the throne called noble frontier drudge and
we both know you are not white
with rage or fury but only from bleeding
too much while trudging behind a wagon and confidentially
did you really conquer Donner Pass with only a handcart?

My mothers nightmares are not yours but just as binding.
If in your sleep you tasted a child's blood upon your teeth
while your chained black hand could not rise
to wipe away his death upon your lips
perhaps you would consider then
why I choose this brick and shitty stone
over the good earth's challenge of green.

Your mothers nightmares are not mine but just as binding.
And we share more than a trap between our legs
where long game howl back and forth across country
finding less than what they bargained for
but more than they ever feared
so dreams or not, I think you will be back soon from Honduras
where the woods are even thicker than in Oregon.
You will see it finally as a choice too
between loving women or loving trees
and if only from the standpoint of free movement
women win
hands down.   [1971]

Hard Love Rock # II

Listen brother love you
love you love you love you dig me
a different colored grave
we are both lying
side by side in the same place
where you put me
down
deeper still
we are
aloneness unresolved by weeping
sacked cities not rebuilt

by slogans
by rhetorical pricks
picking the lock
that has always been
open.

Black is
not beautiful baby
beautiful baby beautiful
lets do it again
It is

not
being screwed twice
at the same time
from on top
as well as
from my side.   [1971]

Love Poem

Speak earth and bless me with what is richest
make sky flow honey out of my hips
rigid as mountains
spread over a valley
carved out by the mouth of rain.

And I knew when I entered her I was
high wind in her forests hollow
fingers whispering sound
honey flowed
from the split cup
impaled on a lance of tongues
on the tips of her breasts on her navel
and my breath
howling into her entrances
through lungs of pain.

Greedy as herring-gulls
or a child
I swing out over the earth
over and over
again.   [1971]

Song For A Thin Sister

Either heard or taught
as girls
we thought
that skinny was funny
or a little bit
silly
and feeling a pull
toward the large and the colorful
I would joke you
when
you grew too thin.

But your new kind of hunger
makes me chilly
like danger
for I see you forever retreating
shrinking
into a stranger
in flight—
and
growing up
black and fat
I was so sure
that skinny was funny
or silly
but always
white.   [1971]

To Marie, In Flight

For women
perspective is more easily maintained.

But something in my body
teaches patience
is no virtue
every month
renews its own destruction
while my blood rages
for proof
or continuity.

Peering out of this
pressured metal cabin
I see my body patterns
repeated on the earth
I hear my blood breath beating
through the dark green places
between the mountain's thrust
without judgment or decision
a valley rhythm captures all.   [1971]

Visit To A City Out Of Time

If a city
takes its rhythms
from the river
that cuts through it
the pulse of the Mississippi
has torn this city
apart.

St. Louis is
somebody's home
and not answering
was
nobody
shoveling snow
because spring would come
some day.

People who live
by rivers
sometimes dream
they are immortal.   [1971]

To My Daughter The Junkie On A Train

Children we have not borne
bedevil us by becoming
themselves

painfully sharp and unavoidable
like a needle in our flesh.

Coming home on the subway from a PTA meeting
of minds committed like murder
or suicide
to their own private struggle
a long-legged girl with a horse in her brain
slumps down beside me
begging to be ridden asleep
for the price of a midnight train
free from desire.
Little girl on the nod
if we are measured by the dreams we avoid
then you are the nightmare
of all sleeping mothers
rocking back and forth
the dead weight of your arms
locked about our necks
heavier than our habit
of looking for reasons.

My corrupt concern will not replace
what you once needed
but I am locked into my own addictions
and offer you my help, one eye
out
for my own station.
Roused and deprived
your costly dream explodes
into a terrible technicolored laughter
at my failure
up and down across the aisle
women avert their eyes
as the other mothers who became useless
curse our children who became junk.   [1972]

A Birthday Memorial To Seventh Street

I

I tarry in days shaped like the high staired street
where I became a woman
between two funeral parlors next door to each other

sharing a dwarf
who kept watch for the hearses
Fox's Bar on the corner
playing happy birthday to a boogie beat
Old slavic men cough in the spring thaw
hawking
painted candles cupcakes fresh eggs
from under their dull green knitted caps
when the right winds blow
the smell of bird seed and malt
from the breweries across the river
stops even our worst hungers.

One crosstown bus each year
carries silence into overcrowded hallways
plucking madmen out of the mailboxes
from under stairwells
from cavorting over rooftops in the full moon
cutting short the mournful songs that used to soothe me
before they would cascade to laughter every afternoon
at four PM
behind a door that never opened
Then masked men in white coats dismount
to take the names of anyone
who has not paid the rent in three months
peel off layers of christmas seals
and batter down the doors to bare apartments
where they duly note the shape of each obscenity
upon the wall
and hunt those tenants down
to make new vacancies.

II

These were some of my lovers who were processed
through the corridors of Bellevue Mattewean Brooklyn State
the Women's House of D. St. Vincent's and the Tombs
to be stapled onto tickets for a one way ride
on the unmarked train that travels
once a year
across the country east to west
filled with New York's rejected lovers
ones who played with all their stakes
who could not win nor learn to lie—
we were much fewer then—
who failed the entry tasks of Seventh Street

and were returned back home
to towns with names like Oblong and Vienna
(called Vyanna)
Cairo Sesser Cave-In-Rock and Legend.
Once a year the train stops unannounced
at midnight
just outside of town
returning the brave of Bonegap and Tuskegee
of Pawnee Falls and Rabbittown
of Anazine and Elegant and Intercourse
leaving them beyond the edge of town
like dried up bones sucked clean of marrow
but rattling with city-like hardness
the soft wood
petrified to stone in Seventh Street.
The train screams
warning the town of coming trouble
then moves on.

III

I walk over Seventh Street
stone at midnight
two years away from forty
and the ghosts of old friends
precede me down the street in welcome
bopping in and out of doorways
with a boogie beat
Freddie sails before me like a made-up bat
his Zorro cape just level with the stoops
he pirouettes upon the garbage cans
a bundle of drugged delusions
hanging from his belt
while Joan with a hand across her throat
sings unafraid of silence anymore
and Marion who lived on the scraps of breath
left in the refuse of strangers
searches the gutter with her nightmare eyes
tripping over the brown girl
young in her eyes and fortune
nimble as birch
and I try to recall her name
as Clement comes
smiling from a distance

his fingers raised in counsel
or in blessing
over us all.

Seventh Street swells into midnight
memory ripe as a bursting grape
my head is a museum
full of other people's eyes
like stones in a dark churchyard
where I kneel praying
that my children
will not die politely
either.   [1972]

One Year To Life
On The Grand Central Shuttle

If we hate the rush hour subways
who ride them every day
why hasn't there been a New York City Subway Riot
some bloody rush-hour revolution
where a snarl
goes on from push to a shove
that does not stop
at the platform's edge
the whining of automated trains
will drown out the screams
of our bloody and releasing testament
to a last chance or hope of change.

But hope is counter-revolutionary.
Pressure cooks
but we have not exploded
flowing in and out instead each day
like a half-digested mass
for a final stake impales our dreams
and watering down each trip's fury
is the someday foolish hope
that at the next stop
some door will open for us
to fresh air and light and home.

When we realize how
much of us is spent
in rush hour subways
underground
no real exit
it will matter less
what token we pay
for change   [1972]

My Fifth Trip To Washington Ended
In Northeast Delaware

FOR CC—RING AROUND CONGRESS JUNE 1972

Halfway between the rain and Washington
as we stopped stuck in the middle of Delaware and a deluge
At least she said
as the muddy waters rose covering our good intentions
At least she said
as we sat stranded neither dry nor high enough
somewhere over a creek very busy becoming a river
somewhere in northeast Delaware
At least she said
as we waited for the engine
to tug us back to where we had started from
and my son complained he could have had more fun
wrapped up in an envelope
At least she said
as the flooded out tracks receded and the waters rose around us
and the children fussed and fretted but were really
very brave about it
and the windows started to leak in on our shoes
and the gum and the games and the New York Times
and the chocolate bars and the toilet paper
all ran out
as the frozen fruit juice melted
and the mayonnaise in the tuna fish went sour
At least she said
as the rain kept falling down
and we couldn't get through to Washington
as we slumped
damp and disappointed in our rumpled up convictions
At least she said
The Indians Aren't Attacking.   [1972]

Separation

The stars dwindle
they will not reward me
even in triumph.

It is possible
to shoot a man
in self defense
and still notice
how his red blood
decorates the snow.   [1972]

Vietnam Addenda

FOR CLIFFORD

Genocide doesn't only mean bombs
at high noon and the cameras
panning in on the ruptured stomach
of somebody else's pubescent daughter.
A small difference in time and space
names that war
while we live
117th street at high noon
powerlessly familiar.
Raped of our children
in silence
we give birth to spots
quickly rubbed out at dawn
on the streets of Jamaica
or left
all the time in the world
for a nightmare of idleness
to turn their hands
against us.   [1972]

The Workers Rose On May Day Or
Postscript To Karl Marx

Down Wall Street
the students marched for peace
Above, construction workers looking on remembered

how it was for them in the old days
before their closed shop white security
and daddy pays the bills
so they climbed down the girders
and taught their sons a lesson
called Marx as a victim of the generation gap
called I grew up the hard way so will you
called
the limits of a sentimental vision.

When the passion play was over
and the dust had cleared on Wall Street
500 Union workers together with police
had mopped up Foley Square
with 2000 of their striking sons
who broke and ran
before their fathers chains.

Look here Karl Marx
the apocalyptic vision of amerika!
Workers rise and win
and have not lost their chains
but swing them
side by side with the billyclubs in blue
securing Wall Street
against the striking students.   [1973]

Keyfood

In the Keyfood Market on Broadway
a woman waits
by the window
daily and patient
the comings and goings of buyers
neatly labeled old
like yesterday's bread
her restless experienced eyes
weigh fears like grapefruit
testing for ripeness.

Once in the market
she was more

comfortable than wealthy
more black than white
more proper than friendly
more rushed than alone
all her powers defined her
like a carefully kneaded loaf
rising and restrained
working and loving
behind secret eyes.

Once she was all
the sums of her knowing
counting on her to sustain them
once she was more
somebody else's mother than mine
now she weighs faces
as once she weighed grapefruit.

Waiting
she does not count her change
Her lonely eyes measure
all who enter the market
are they new
are they old
enough
can they buy each other?   [1973]

A Trip On The Staten Island Ferry

Dear Jonno
there are pigeons who nest
on the Staten Island Ferry
and raise their young
between the moving decks
and never touch
ashore.

Every voyage is a journey.

Cherish this city
left you by default
include it in your daydreams

there are still
secrets
in the streets
even I have not discovered
who knows
if the old men
who shine shoes on the Staten Island Ferry
carry their world
in a box slung across their shoulders
if they share their lunch
with birds
flying back and forth
upon an endless journey
if they ever find their way
back home.   [1973]

Now

Woman power
is
Black power
is
Human power
is
always feeling
my heart beats
as my eyes open
as my hands move
as my mouth speaks

I am
are you

Ready.   [1973]

Memorial III
From a Phone Booth on Broadway

Some time turns inside out
and the whole day collapses into
a desperate search

for a telephone booth that works
for
   quick quick
               I must call you
who has not spoken inside my head
for over a year
if this phone burrs
long enough
pressed up against my ear
you will blossom back into sound
you will answer
must answer
answer me answer me
answer goddammit
answer
      please
answer
this is the last time
I shall ever call
you.   [1973]

And Don't Think I Won't Be Waiting

I am supposed to say
it doesn't matter look me up some
time when you're in my neighborhood
needing
a drink or some books good talk
a quick dip before lunch—
but I never was one
for losing
what i couldn't afford
from the beginning
your richness made my heart
burn like a roman candle.

Now I don't mind
your hand on my face like fire
like a slap
turned inside out
quick as a caress
but I'm warning you

this time
you will not slip away
under a covering cloud
of my tears.   [1973]

For My Singing Sister

Little sister, not all black
people are all ready
people
are not always black
people
finding them
selves close
to how they see
themselves
being most important.

I see your friends are
young skinny girls sometimes
tall sometimes slight sometimes
beige and neutral or mean or honest or weak
sometimes warm some
times even you
haunted by fat black women who alter
like dreams in a shattered mirror
becoming
sometimes tall sometimes slight sometimes
beige and neutral or mean
honest or weak sometimes warm
sometimes even you
hiding in a bloodbath of color
as you slice up love
on the edge of your little mirrors
making smaller
but not safer
images of your sun.

Cherish your nightmare
sister
or under a cloak of respect
the fat black witch

may be buried
a silver stake
through your heart.   [1973]

Monkeyman

There is a strange man attached to my backbone
who thinks he can sap me or break me
if he bleaches out my son my water my fire
if he confuses my tongue by shitting his symbols
into my words.

Every day I walk out of my house
with this curious weight on my back
peering out from between my ear and my shoulder
and each time I move my head
his breath smells like a monkey
he tugs at my short hairs
trying to make me look
into shop windows
trying to make me buy
wigs and girdles and polyutherane pillows
and whenever
I walk through Harlem
he whispers—"be careful—
"our nigger will get us!"

I used to pretend
I did not hear him.   [1972]

Oya

God of my father discovered at midnight
my mother asleep on her thunders
my father
returning at midnight
out of tightening circles of anger
out of days' punishment
the inelegant safety of power
Now midnight empties your house of bravado

and passion sleeps like a mist
outside desire
your strength splits like a melon
dropped on your prisoners floor
midnight glows
like a jeweled love
at the core of the broken fruit.

My mother is sleeping.
Hymns of dream lie like bullets
in her nights weapons
the sacred steeples
of nightmare are secret and hidden
in the disguise of fallen altars
I too shall learn how to conquer yes
Yes yes god
damned
I love you
now free me
quickly
before I destroy us.   [1973]

The Brown Menace Or
Poem To The Survival Of Roaches

Call me
your deepest urge
toward survival
call me
and my brothers and sisters
in the sharp smell of your refusal
call me
roach and presumptuous
nightmare on your white pillow
your itch to destroy
the indestructible
part of yourself.

Call me
your own determination
in the most detestable shape
you can become

friend of your own image
within me
I am you
in your most deeply cherished nightmare
scuttling through the painted cracks
you create to admit me
into your kitchens
into your fearful midnights
into your values at noon
in your most secret places
with hate
you learn to honor me
by imitation
as I alter—
through your greedy preoccupations
through your kitchen wars
through your poisonous refusal—
to survive.

To survive.
To survive.   [1973]

Sacrifice

The only hungers left
are the hungers allowed us.

By the light of our sacred street lamps
by whatever maps we are sworn to follow
pleasure will betray us
unless we do what we must do
without
wanting to do it
feel the enemy stone give way in retreat
without pleasure or satisfaction
we look the other way
as our dreams come true
as our bloody hands move over history
writing
we have come
we have done
what we come to do.

Pulling down statues of rock from their high places
we must level the expectation
upon which they stand
waiting for us
to fulfill their image
waiting
for our feet to replace them.
Unless we refuse to sleep
even one night in houses of marble
the sight of our children's false pleasure
will undo us
for our children have grown
in the shadow of what was
the shape of marble
between their eyes and the sun
but we do not wish to stand like great marble statues
between our children's eyes
and their sun.

Learning all
we can use
only what is vital
The only sacrifice of worth
is the sacrifice of desire.

[1973]

Blackstudies

I

A chill wind sweeps the high places.
On the ground I watch bearers of wood
carved in the image of old and mistaken gods
labor in search of weapons against the blind dancers
who balance great dolls on their shoulders
as they scramble over the same earth
searching for food.

In a room on the 17th floor my spirit is choosing
I am afraid of speaking
the truth
in a room on the 17th floor
my body is dreaming

it sits
bottom pinned to a table
eating perpetual watermelon inside my own head
while young girls assault my door
with curse rags
stiff with their mothers old secrets
covering up their new promise
with old desires no longer their need
with old satisfactions they never enjoyed
outside my door they are waiting
with questions that feel like judgments
when they are unanswered.

The palms of my hands have black marks running across them.
So are signed markers of myth
who are sworn through our blood to give
legend
children will come to understand
to speak out living words like this poem
that knits truth into fable
to leave my story behind
though I fall through cold wind condemned
to nursing old gods for a new heart
debtless and without color
while my flesh is covered by mouths
whose noise keeps my real wants secret.

I do not want to lie. I have loved other
tall young women deep into their color
who now cawl over a bleached earth
bent into questionmarks
ending a sentence of men
who pretended to be brave.
Even this
can be an idle defense
protecting the lies I am trying to reject.

I am afraid
that the mouths I feed will turn against me
will refuse to swallow in the silence
I am warning them to avoid
I am afraid
they will kernel me out like a walnut

extracting the nourishing seed
as my husk strains their lips
with the mixed colors of my pain.

While I sit choosing the voice
in which my children hear my prayers
above the wind
they will follow the black roads out of my hands
unencumbered by the weight of guilty secrets
by the weight of my remembered sorrows
they will use my legends to shape their own language
and make it ruler
measuring the distance between my hungers
and their own purpose.
I am afraid
They will discard my most ancient nightmares
where the fallen gods became demon
instead of dust.

II

Just before light devils woke me
trampling my flesh into fruit
that would burst in the sun
until I came to despise every evening
fearing a strange god at the fall of each night
and when my mother punished me
by sending me to bed without my prayers
I had no names for darkness.

I do not know whose words protected me
whose tales or tears prepared me
for this trial on the 17th floor
I do not know whose legends blew
through my mothers furies
but somehow they fell through my sleeping lips
like the juice of forbidden melons
and the little black seeds were sown
throughout my heart
like closed and waiting eyes
and although demons rode me
until I rose up a child of morning
deep roads sprouted over the palms
of my hidden fists
dark and growing.

III

Chill winds swirl around these high blank places.
It is the time when the bearer of hard news
is destroyed for the message
when it is heard.
A.B. is a poet who says our people
fear our own beauty
has not made us hard enough
to survive victory
but he too has written his children upon women
I hope with love.

I bear mine alone in the mouth of the enemy
upon a desk on the 17th floor
swept bare by cold winds
bright as neon.

IV

Their demon father rode me just before daylight
I learned his tongue as he reached
for my hands at dawn
before he could touch the palms of my hands
to devour my children
I learned his language
I ate him
and left his bones mute in the noon sun.

Now all the words in my legend come garbled
except anguish.
Visions of chitterlings I never ate
strangle me in a nightmare of leaders
at crowded meetings to study our problems
I move awkward and ladylike
through four centuries of unused bathtubs
that never smile
not even an apologetic grin
I worry on nationalist holidays
make a fetish of lateness
with limp unbelieved excuses
shunning the use of pronouns
as an indirect assault
what skin I have left
unbetrayed by scouring
uncovered by mouths that shriek

but do not speak my real wants
glistens and twinkles blinding all beholders
"But I just washed them, Mommy!"

Only the black marks on my hands itch and flutter
shredding my words and wherever they fall
the earth springs up denials
that I pay for
only the dark roads over my palms
wait for my voice
to follow.

V

The chill wind is beating down from the high places.
My students wait outside my door
searching condemning listening
for what I am sworn to tell them
for what they least want to hear
clogging the only exit from the 17th floor
begging in their garbled language
beyond judgment or understanding
"oh speak to us now mother for soon
we will not need you
only your memory
teaching us questions."

Stepping into my self
I open the door
and leap groundward
wondering
what shall they carve for weapons
what shall they grow for food.   [1973]

New Poems

The Evening News

First rule of the road: attend quiet victims first.

I am kneading my bread Winnie Mandela
while children who sing in the streets of Soweto
are jailed for inciting to riot
the moon in Soweto is mad
is bleeding my sister into the earth
is mixing her seed with the vultures'
greeks reap her like olives out of the trees
she is skimmed like salt
from the skin of a hungry desert
while the Ganvie fisherwomen with milk-large breasts
hide a fish with the face of a small girl
in the prow of their boats.

Winnie Mandela I am feeling your face
with pain of my crippled fingers
our children are escaping their births
in the streets of Soweto and Brooklyn
(what does it mean
our wars
being fought by our children?)

Winnie Mandela our names are like olives, salt, sand
the opal, amber, obsidian that hide their shape well.
We have never touched shaven foreheads together
yet how many of our sisters' and daughters' bones
whiten in secret
whose names we have not yet spoken
whose names we have never spoken
I have never heard their names spoken.

*Second rule of the road: any wound will stop bleeding if
you press down hard enough.*

Za Ki Tan Ke Parlay Lot*

Oh za ki tan ke parlay lot
you who hear tell the others
there is no metaphor for blood

* Called in the streets of Carriacou, West Indies, before a funeral or burial.

flowing from children
these are your deaths
or your judgments
za ki tan ke parlay lot
you who hear tell the others
this is not some othsr cities' trial
your locks are no protection
hate chips at your front doors like flint
flames creep beneath them
my children are resting in question
and your tomorrows flicker
a face without eyes
without future
za ki tan ke parlay lot
whose visions lie dead in the alleys
dreams bagged like old leaves
anger shorn of promise
you are drowning in my children's blood
without metaphor
oh you who hear tell the others
za ki tan ke parlay lot.

Afterimages

I

However the image enters
its force remains within
my eyes
rockstrewn caves where dragonfish evolve
wild for life, relentless and acquisitive
learning to survive
where there is no food
my eyes are always hungry
and remembering
however the image enters
its force remains.
A white woman stands bereft and empty
a black boy hacked into a murderous lesson
recalled in me forever
like a lurch of earth on the edge of sleep
etched into my visions
food for dragonfish that learn
to live upon whatever they must eat
fused images beneath my pain.

II

The Pearl River floods through the streets of Jackson
A Mississippi summer televised.
Trapped houses kneel like sinners in the rain
a white woman climbs from her roof to a passing boat
her fingers tarry for a moment on the chimney
now awash
tearless and no longer young, she holds
a tattered baby's blanket in her arms.
In a flickering afterimage of the nightmare rain
a microphone
thrust up against her flat bewildered words
  "we jest come from the bank yestiddy
    borrowing money to pay the income tax
    now everything's gone. I never knew
    it could be so hard."
Despair weighs down her voice like Pearl River mud
caked around the edges
her pale eyes scanning the camera for help or explanation
unanswered
she shifts her search across the watered street, dry-eyed
    "hard, but not this hard."
Two tow-headed children hurl themselves against her
hanging upon her coat like mirrors
until a man with ham-like hands pulls her aside
snarling "She ain't got nothing more to say!"
and that lie hangs in his mouth
like a shred of rotting meat.

III

I inherited Jackson, Mississippi.
For my majority it gave me Emmett Till
his 15 years puffed out like bruises
on plump boy-cheeks
his only Mississippi summer
whistling a 21 gun salute to Dixie
as a white girl passed him in the street
and he was baptized my son forever
in the midnight waters of the Pearl.

His broken body is the afterimage of my 21st year
when I walked through a northern summer
my eyes averted
from each corner's photographies
newspapers protest posters magazines

Police Story, Confidential, True
the avid insistence of detail
pretending insight or information
the length of gash across the dead boy's loins
his grieving mother's lamentation
the severed lips, how many burns
his gouged out eyes
sewed shut upon the screaming covers
louder than life
all over
the veiled warning, the secret relish
of a black child's mutilated body
fingered by street-corner eyes
bruise upon livid bruise
and wherever I looked that summer
I learned to be at home with children's blood
with savored violence
with pictures of black broken flesh
used, crumpled, and discarded
lying amid the sidewalk refuse
like a raped woman's face.

A black boy from Chicago
whistled on the streets of Jackson, Mississippi
testing what he'd been taught was a manly thing to do
his teachers
ripped his eyes out his sex his tongue
and flung him to the Pearl weighted with stone
in the name of white womanhood
they took their aroused honor
back to Jackson
and celebrated in a whorehouse
the double ritual of white manhood
confirmed.

IV

*"If earth and air and water do not judge them who are
we to refuse a crust of bread?"*

Emmett Till rides the crest of the Pearl, whistling
24 years his ghost lay like the shade of a raped woman
and a white girl has grown older in costly honor
(what did she pay to never know its price?)
now the Pearl River speaks its muddy judgment
and I can withhold my pity and my bread.

"Hard, but not this hard."
Her face is flat with resignation and despair
with ancient and familiar sorrows
a woman surveying her crumpled future
as the white girl besmirched by Emmett's whistle
never allowed her own tongue
without power or conclusion
unvoiced
she stands adrift in the ruins of her honor
and a man with an executioner's face
pulls her away.

Within my eyes
the flickering afterimages of a nightmare rain
a woman wrings her hands
beneath the weight of agonies remembered
I wade through summer ghosts
betrayed by vision
hers and my own
becoming dragonfish to survive
the horrors we are living
with tortured lungs
adapting to breathe blood.

A woman measures her life's damage
my eyes are caves, chunks of etched rock
tied to the ghost of a black boy
whistling
crying and frightened
her tow-headed children cluster
like little mirrors of despair
their father's hands upon them
and soundlessly
a woman begins to weep.   [1981]

A Poem For Women In Rage

A killing summer heat wraps up the city
emptied of all who are not bound to stay
a black woman waits for a white woman
leans against the railing in the Upper Westside street
at intermission

the distant sounds of Broadway dim to lulling
until I can hear the voice of sparrows
like a promise I await
the woman I love
our slice of time
a place beyond the city's pain.

In the corner phonebooth a woman
glassed in by reflections of the street between us
her white face dangles
a tapestry of disasters seen
through a veneer of order
her mouth drawn like an ill-used roadmap
to eyes without core, a bottled heart
impeccable credentials of old pain.

The veneer cracks open
hate launches through the glaze into my afternoon
our eyes touch like hot wire
and the street snaps into nightmare
a woman with white eyes is clutching
a bottle of Fleischmann's gin
is fumbling at her waistband
is pulling a butcher knife from her ragged pants
her hand arcs backward "You Black Bitch!"
the heavy blade spins out toward me
slow motion
years of fury surge upward like a wall
I do not hear it
clatter to the pavement at my feet.

A gear of ancient nightmare churns
swift in familiar dread and silence
but this time I am awake, released
I smile. Now. This time is
my turn.
I bend to the knife my ears blood-drumming
across the street my lover's voice
the only moving sound within white heat
"Don't touch it!"
I straighten, weaken, then start down again
hungry for resolution
simple as anger and so close at hand

my fingers reach for the familiar blade
the known grip of wood against my palm
I have held it to the whetstone
a thousand nights for this
escorting fury through my sleep
like a cherished friend
to wake in the stink of rage
beside the sleep-white face of love.

The keen steel of a dreamt knife
sparks honed from the whetted edge with a tortured shriek
between my lover's voice and the grey spinning
a choice of pain or fury
slashing across judgment like a crimson scar
I could open her up to my anger
with a point sharpened upon love.

In the deathland my lover's voice
fades
like the roar of a train derailed
on the other side of a river
every white woman's face I love
and distrust is upon it
eating green grapes from a paper bag
marking yellow exam-books tucked into a manilla folder
orderly as the last thought before death
I throw the switch.
Through screams of crumpled steel
I search the wreckage for a ticket of hatred
my lover's voice
calling
a knife at her throat.

In this steaming aisle of the dead
I am weeping
to learn the names of those streets
my feet have worn thin with running
and why they will never serve me
nor ever lead me home.
"Don't touch it!" she cries
I straighten myself
in confusion
a drunken woman is running away

down the Westside street
my lover's voice moves me
to a shadowy clearing.

Corralled in fantasy
the woman with white eyes has vanished
to become her own nightmare
a french butcher blade hangs in my house
love's token
I remember this knife
it carved its message into my sleeping
she only read its warning
written upon my face.

[1981]

October

Spirits
of the abnormally born
live on in water
of the heroically dead
in the entrails of snake.
Now I span my days like a wild bridge
swaying in place
caught between poems like a vise
I am finishing my piece of this bargain
and how shall I return?

Seboulisa, mother of power
keeper of birds
fat and beautiful
give me the strength of your eyes
to remember
what I have learned
help me to attend with passion
these tasks at my hand for doing.

Carry my heart to some shore
that my feet will not shatter
do not let me pass away
before I have a name

for this tree
under which I am lying.
Do not let me die
still
needing to be stranger.   [1980]

Sister, Morning Is A Time For Miracles

A core of the conversations we never had
lies in the distance
between your wants and mine
a piece of each
buried beneath the wall that separates
our sameness
a talisman of birth
hidden at the root of your mother's spirit
my mother's furies.

Now reaching for you with my sad words
between sleeping and waking
a runic stone speaks
what is asked for is often destroyed
by the very words that seek it
like dew in the early morning
dissolving the tongue of salt as well as its thirst
and I call you secret names of praise and fire
that sound like your birthright
but are not the names of a friend
while you hide from me under 100 excuses
lying like tombstones along the road
between your house and mine.

I could accept any blame I understood
but picking over the fresh and possible loneliness
of this too-early morning
I find the relics of my history
fossilized into a prison
where I learn to make love forever
better than how to make friends
where you are encased like a half-stoned peach

in the rigid art of your healing
and in case you have ever tried to reach me
and I couldn't hear you
these words are in place of the dead air
still between us:

A memorial to conversations we won't be having
to laughter shared and important
as the selves we helped make real
but also to the dead
revelations we buried still-born
in the refuse of fear and silence
and your remembered eyes
which don't meet mine anymore.

(I never intended to let you slip through my fingers
nor to purchase your interest ever again
like the desire of a whore
who yawns behind her upturned hand
pretending a sigh of pleasure
and I have had that, too, already.)

Once I thought when I opened my eyes we would move
into a freer and more open country
where the sun could illuminate our different desires
and the fresh air do us honor for who we were
yet I have awakened at 4 A.M. with a ribald joke to tell you
and found I had lost the name of the street
where you hid under an assumed name
and I knew I would have to bleed again
in order to find you
but just once
in the possibilities of this too-early morning
I wanted you
to talk
not as a healer
bur as a lonely woman
talking to a friend.   [1979]

Need: A Choral Of Black Women's Voices

FOR PATRICIA COWAN AND BOBBIE JEAN GRAHAM
AND THE HUNDREDS OF OTHER MANGLED BLACK WOMEN
WHOSE NIGHTMARES INFORM THEM MY WORDS

> *tattle tale tit*
> *your tongue will be slit*
> *and every little boy in town*
> *shall have a little bit.*
> —NURSERY RHYME

I

I: This woman is Black
so her blood is shed into silence
this woman is Black
so her death falls to earth
like the drippings of birds
to be washed away with silence and rain.

P.C.: For a long time after the baby came
I didn't go out at all
and it got to be really lonely.
Then Bubba started asking about his father
I wanted to connect with the blood again
thought maybe I'd meet somebody
and we could move on together
help make the dream real.
An ad in the paper said
"Black actress needed
to audition in a play by Black playwright."
I was anxious to get back to work
thought this might be a good place to start
so on the way home from school with Bubba
I answered the ad.
He put a hammer through my head.

B.J.G.: If you are hit in the middle of your body
by a ten-ton truck
your caved-in chest bears the mark of a tire
and your liver pops
like a rubber ball.
If you are knocked down by boulders
from a poorly graded hill
your dying is stamped by the rockprint
upon your crushed body

by the impersonal weight of it all
while life drips out through your liver
smashed by the mindless stone.
When your boyfriend methodically beats you to death
in the alley behind your apartment
and the neighbors pull down their windowshades
because they don't want to get involved
the police call it a crime of passion
not a crime of hatred
but I still died
of a lacerated liver
and a man's heel
imprinted upon my chest.

I: Dead Black women haunt the black maled streets
    paying the cities' secret and familiar tithe of blood
    burn blood beat blood cut blood
    seven year old child rape victim blood blood
    of a sodomized grandmother blood blood
    on the hands of my brother blood
    and his blood clotting in the teeth of strangers
    as women we were meant to bleed
    but not this useless blood
    my blood each month a memorial
    to my unspoken sisters falling
    like red drops to the asphalt
    I am not satisfied to bleed
    as a quiet symbol for no one's redemption
    why is it our blood
    that keeps these cities fertile?

    I do not even know all their names.
    My sisters deaths are not noteworthy
    nor threatening enough to decorate the evening news
    not important enough to be fossilized
    between the right-to-life pickets
    and the San Francisco riots for gay liberation
    blood blood of my sisters fallen in this bloody war
    with no names no medals no exchange of prisoners
    no packages from home
    no time off for good behavior
    no victories no victors

B.J.G.: Only us
    kept afraid to walk out into moonlight

lest we touch our power
only us
kept afraid to speak out
lest our tongues be slit
for the witches we are
our chests crushed
by the foot of a brawny acquaintance
and a ruptured liver bleeding life onto the stones.

ALL: And how many other deaths
      do we live through daily
      pretending
      we are alive?

II

P.C.: What terror embossed my face onto your hatred
       what ancient and unchallenged enemy
       took on my flesh within your eyes
       came armed against you
       with laughter and a hopeful art
       my hair catching the sunlight
       my small son eager to see his mother at work?
       Now my blood stiffens in the cracks
       of your fingers raised to wipe
       a half-smile from your lips.
       In this picture of you
       the face of a white policeman
       bends
       over my bleeding son
       decaying into my brother
       who stalked me with a singing hammer.

B.J.G.: And what do you need me for, brother,
         to move for you, feel for you, die for you?
         You have a grave need for me
         but your eyes are thirsty for vengance
         dressed in the easiest blood
         and I am closest.

P.C.: When you opened my head with your hammer
       did the boogie stop in your brain
       the beat go on
       the terror run out of you like curdled fury
       a half-smile upon your lips?
       And did your manhood lay in my skull like a netted fish

or did it spill out like blood
like impotent fury off the tips of your fingers
as your sledgehammer clove my bone to let the light out
did you touch it as it flew away?

ALL: Borrowed hymns veil the misplaced hatred
saying you need me you need me you need me
like a broken drum
calling me black goddess black hope black strength
black mother
you touch me
and I die in the alleys of Boston
with a stomach stomped through the small of my back
a hammered-in skull in Detroit
a ceremonial knife through my grandmother's used vagina
my burned body hacked to convenience in a vacant lot
I lie in midnight blood like a rebel city
bombed into false submission
and our enemies still sit in power
and judgment
over us all.

P.C.: *I need you.*
was there no place left
to plant your hammer
spend anger rest horror
no other place to dig for your manhood
except in my woman's brain?

B.J.G.: Do you need me submitting to terror at nightfall
to chop into bits and stuff warm into plastic bags
near the neck of the Harlem River
and they found me there
swollen with your need
do you need me to rape in my seventh year
till blood breaks the corners of my child's mouth
and you explain I was being seductive

ALL: Do you need me to print on our children
the destruction our enemies imprint upon you
like a Mack truck or an avalanche
destroying us both
carrying home their hatred
you are re-learning my value
in an enemy coin.

III

I: I am wary of need
that tastes like destruction.
I am wary of need that tastes like destruction.
Who ever learns to love me
from the mouth of my enemies
walks the edge of my world
like a phantom in a crimson cloak
and the dreambooks speak of money
but my eyes say death.

The simplest part of this poem
is the truth in each one of us
to which it is speaking.
How much of this truth can I bear to see
and still live
unblinded?
How much of this pain
can I use?

ALL: *"We cannot live without our lives."*
"We cannot live without our lives."   [1979]

NOTES

Patricia Cowan, 21, bludgeoned to death in Detroit, 1978.

Bobbie Jean Graham, 34, beaten to death in Boston, 1979. One of 12 black women murdered within a 3 month period in that city.

"We cannot live without our lives" from a poem by Barbara Deming.